Eyewitness Accounts of the American Revolution

Letters of
Eliza Wilkinson
Edited by Caroline Gilman

The New York Times & Arno Press

LETTERS OF ELIZA WILKINSON.

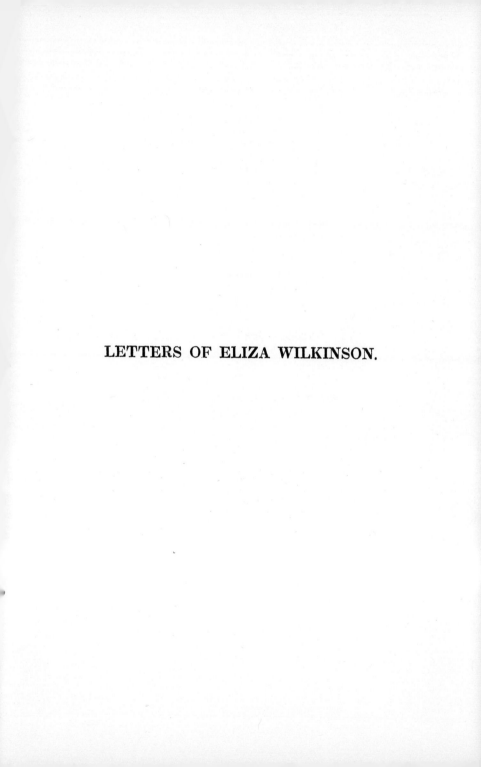

LETTERS

OF

ELIZA WILKINSON,

DURING THE

INVASION AND POSSESSION OF CHARLESTOWN, S. C. BY THE
BRITISH IN THE REVOLUTIONARY WAR.

ARRANGED FROM THE ORIGINAL MANUSCRIPTS,

BY

CAROLINE GILMAN.

NEW-YORK:

PUBLISHED BY SAMUEL COLMAN,

NO. 8 ASTOR HOUSE.

BROADWAY.

1839.

NEW-YORK:
Printed by SCATCHERD & ADAMS,
No. 38 Gold Street.

PREFACE.

Few records exist of American women either before or during the war of the revolution. Those
perpetuated by history, though honorable, particularly to the Southern States, want the charm of person-
al narration. To those of us who dwell among her
kindred, Eliza Wilkinson's letters present a most liv-
ing picture ; and they cannot fail to excite public interest at a period, when such anxiety is abroad to
gather every relic of our part history before it floats
away down the stream of time.

At the season of writing her letters, Mrs. Wilkinson was a young and beautiful widow ; her hand-
writing, where it is not defaced by the damps of time,
is clear and feminine. The letters were copied by her-
self into a blank quarto book, on which the extrava-
gant sale-price marks one of the features of the times.

Yonge's Island is about thirty miles southwardly
from Charlestown, and is separated from the main
land by a small creek, over which there is a cause-

way. " The Sands," near which she lost her shoes
in flight, still retain the name. The avenue to
which she alludes remains, though a parallel one
has been formed by the division of the estate among
descendants. Nothing can exceed the beauty of this
approach, it being a hedge of the Cherokee Rose
three miles in length. The old family mansion has
been removed, but the burial-ground is held sacred.

CONTENTS.

LETTERS, &c.

LETTER I.

Introductory remarks. British outrages at the North. A Negro woman announces the approach of the enemy within five miles of Yonge's Island. Terror of the women. Mrs. Wilkinson goes to Wadmalaw. Distress at leaving her old father. Meets a boat-load of fugitive women and children on their way to Charlestown.

To Miss M—— P——.

YONGE'S ISLAND, 1782.

As I mean never to forget the *loving-kindness and ten-der mercies* of the renowned Britons while among us, in the ever-memorable year 1779, I shall transmit you a brief account of their *polite* behavior to my Father and family, where you will find me sufficiently punished for being something of an unbeliever heretofore. You

2

know we had always heard most terrible accounts of
the actions of the British troops at the northward;
but, (fool that I was,) I thought they must be exaggerat-
ed, for I could not believe that a nation so famed for
humanity, and many other virtues, should, in so short a
time, divest themselves of even the least trace of what
they once were.

Surely, said I, they can't, in so short a time, have
commenced savages, and lost those virtues which have
distinguished them from other nations.   Yet, sometimes,
when I heard fresh accounts of their cruelty to our
Northern brethren when in their power, I could not re-
press my indignation against the barbarous, hard-hearted
Britons, (how changed their character!) and believed, or
almost believed, what I had heard of them.   I say *almost*,
for I was so infatuated with what I had formerly heard
and read of Englishmen, that I thought humanity, and
every manly sentiment, were their inherent qualities ;—
though I cannot but say that, much as I had admired
the former lustre of the British character, my soul
shrunk from the thought of having any communication
with a people who had left their homes with a direct intention to imbrue their hands in the blood of my beloved
countrymen, or deprive them of their birthright, Liberty

and property. The thought alarmed me, shocked me. I began to look on the Britons in earnest as enemies.

At length I heard they had got possession of the Georgia State, and used the inhabitants cruelly, paying no respect to age or sex; but then, again, I heard to the contrary, that their behavior to the ladies was unexceptionable. I did not know what to think, much less what to do, should they invade our State, which was daily expected.

Thousands would I have given to have been in any part of the globe where I might not see them, or to have been secure from the impending evils, which were ready to burst over our heads.

I was in Charlestown when we heard that a large party of them had landed somewhere near Beaufort. I saw several detachments of our Southern troops leave town to oppose the invaders of their country. They marched with the greatest alacrity imaginable, not regarding the weather, though the rain poured down incessantly upon them. I cannot describe my feelings upon this sight—gratitude, affection, and pity for my countrymen filled my heart and my eyes, which pursued them until out of sight, and then every good wish attended them. However, it was not long before our little band

of patriots returned to their homes in triumph, excepting
a few, who had sealed the cause with their blood. Peace
to their ashes, and everlasting happiness to their immor-
tal part.

" Well have they perished—for in fight they fell." I
think old Priam says this of his sons, who fell at the
siege of Troy. But who can forbear the tear of sympathy for the distressed families, who are left behind to
mourn the fall of those they highly valued, and from
whom they derived their support? Pitiable reflection!
"How seldom do the rich feel the distresses of the poor,
and in the midst of conquest and acclamation, who re-
gardeth the tears and afflictions of those who have lost
their friends in the public ?"

Now, the time drew near when this State was to have
her day of suffering in sympathy with her sister States.
Oh, how I dreaded the approaching enemy ! I had
thoughts (with my other friends,) to go higher up the
country to avoid them ; but as my Father, with many
others of my relations, had not conveniences ready to carry off their effects with them, and as the enemy aproach-
ed rapidly, they agreed to stay. It was a melancholy
sight to see such crowds of helpless, distressed women,
weeping for husbands, brothers, or other near relations

and friends, who were they knew not where, whether dead or alive. When the enemy were at Ashepoo, or somewhere thereabouts, my sister and sister-in-law were then at my Father's, when one Sunday morning a negro wench, who had been out visiting, came running home in a violent hurry, informing us that a party of British horse were then at Mr. W.'s, not above five or six miles from us.

A boy on the road had informed our servant of the approach of the enemy. This created such confusion and distress among us all as I cannot describe. A boat was immediately pushed off. My sister Yonge, my sister Smilie, and myself, were desirous of putting the evil day afar off; so we went over the river to Mr. Smilie's. Father and Mother ventured to stay at home. Melancholy were the adieus on both sides. We had got but a small distance from the house when we met another lady, who, upon receiving the like information, had walked about two miles, (if not more,) to Father's. She joined us and away we went, often looking back, with watery eyes, to our Father's dwelling, thinking, at the same time, that in all probability, even while we were looking, he might be suffering all the insults and cruelties that a remorseless gang of barbarians could inflict. These

2*

thoughts drew sighs and tears from us; however, we made the best of it, and endeavored to console one another the best we could; but poor was that consolation, you may think.

We had but just got over, when a scene presented itself to us, enough to move the hardest heart in the British army could they have seen it. This was a large boat-load of women and children on their way to Charlestown, as that place promised more safety than any other. They called at Mr. Smilie's, and staid a day or two. I pitied them all greatly, (though we were much in the same situation;) one lady especially, who had seven children, and one of them but a fortnight old; thus, in her weakly situation, to venture her life and that of her babe, rather than fall into the hands of an enemy, whose steps have been marked with cruelty and oppression. Surely, if the British knew the misery they occasion, they would abate their rigor, and blush to think that the name of Englishman, (once so famous among the Fair,) should now produce terror and dismay in every female breast. I'll now lay by my pen—Farewell.

I will proceed by and bye with my narrative, for the various scenes I've been witness to are so much in my head, that I shall not want subjects to employ my pen for some time.

Once more adieu.

ELIZA W.

LETTER II.

I RESUME the pen—but don't smile at my historical
manner of relating matters of fact.   I choose to be me-
thodical, my dear, and begin with my fears and appre-
hensions, and you shall have them all verified in due
time and place.

We staid over at Wadmalaw for some time.   The enemy were all around my Father's, but had not as yet been
so *complaisant* as to visit him.   The whole country was
open to them.   Nothing but women, a few aged gentle-
men, and (shame to tell) some skulking varlets, inhabited it ; the latter, indeed, inhabited the dark recesses of
the woods more than anywhere else, probably thinking
so many huge trees might deaden a shot, should it happen to pass that way.

The poor women were in the greatest distress imaginable. There was no hearing from Charlestown, where all our relations were ready to defend the town in case of an attack, and waiting for General Lincoln. Him, too, we could hear nothing about, unless from disaffected people and negroes, and they were always the most disheartening accounts that we did hear. Once we heard that the enemy had surrounded the town; that they were at Wando, James's Island, and I don't know how many more islands; however, it seemed that they had cut off all means of provision getting to town, and that our troops there were in a starving condition.

Such reports as these were constantly circulated about, and half distracted the people. Some believed, others disbelieved. I was one of the unbelievers. However, it was the constant topic of conversation. Some said one thing, some another; and depend upon it, never were greater politicians than the several knots of ladies, who met together. All trifling discourse of fashions, and such low little chat was thrown by, and we commenced perfect statesmen. Indeed, I don't know but if we had taken a little pains, we should have been qualified for prime ministers, so well could we discuss several important matters in hand.

Many days were we in this cruel suspense, lamenting the situation we were in, and the report concerning our brethren in Charlestown.   The few persons who were at Wadmalaw began to waver ; some insisted it would be rash and foolish for them to make any resistance ; however, they turned out to watch the enemy's movements, and I believe had a shot or two at some of them ; but finding that they began to move in large parties to James's and John's Islands, they all repaired to their homes to wait the event.   I can't say all, either ; some few, whose bodies were inhabited by *true American souls,* stood in opposition to the last, until they were unfortunately surprised one rainy night, when they were keeping guard, and fell into the enemy's hands.

When I found how affairs stood in Wadmalaw, I took a melancholy leave of my sister, Mrs. Smilie, and returned to my Father's.   But still I could hear nothing of our long-looked-for General.   It was moving—in the highest degree distressing, to hear the cry re-echoed from every trembling mouth, " Where is Lincoln ?" but rather, said I, where's the *Lord God of Israel ?*   Will he indeed deliver us into the hands of these Philistines ? No ; the upholding hand of God was visible ; for, though the whole country was open to the enemy, nothing but

women and children left unprotected at home ; husbands, fathers, brothers, friends, and countrymen far
away, where we could not have the least information of
them ; yet we did not wholly despond, we trusted in more
than feeble flesh and blood, and, though our troubles were
great, our dependence was not in vain.

At last my brothers, with the Willtown hunters, arrived from Charlestown. Judge of our joy, augmented, too,
by their assuring us that they had heard from Gen.
Lincoln ; that he was hurrying to our assistance, and
would soon be with us ! How we congratulated one
another on these tidings ; we could now converse with
cheerfulness, and take pleasure in each other's company ;
the gloom, which had so lately darkened every object,
seemed dispelled, and hope, smiling hope, succeeded.

> " Hope, of all passions, most befriends us here ;
> Passions of higher note befriend us less.
> Joy has her tears,—and transport has her death :
> Hope, like a cordial, innocent, though strong,
> Our hearts at once enlivens, and serenes."

Hope seems implanted in us. It is the foundation of
happiness. The great Creator, knowing our weak, des-
ponding natures, has endowed us with it to soothe, sof-
ten, and heal the wounds of keen distress and anguish,
and make us bear with fortitude the many misfortunes

which attend humanity. Without this gentle, healing
passion, dreadful despair would take possession of us ;
and then, oh, what then, but misery unutterable ! What
makes the infernal regions so hideous, but the loss of
hope ? I have never considered this same Hope, nor
seen it in the light I have lately done. It makes a kind
of paradise on earth. Great, then, must be its qualities,
which can find happiness in a soil whose chief produce
is sorrow.

Farewell ! my dear Mary. I am in a moralizing hu-
mor, so I will lay down my pen, and induce reflection
for awhile. I am very busy just now, so that my hands
and thoughts will both be employed in work and con-
templation. You will laugh, and say I am a contempla-
tive mortal. Yes, by fits and starts ; a philosopher too,
in my way ! Not of the sect of Stoics though. I do
most heartily despise those insensible beings. They
are a void in creation. Once more, adieu—Heaven
bless you.

Eliza W.

LETTER III.

Thoughts on peace. Mrs. Wilkinson retreats again from the river plantation at the approach of the enemy. Affecting interview with passing soldiers. The enemy kept off by a negro. British soldiers. A visit of plunder and insult on the 2d of June. Another on the 3d. A party of M'Girth's men arrive at the plantation.

> " Sweet is the breath of morn, her rising sweet,
>   With charm of earliest birds ; pleasant the sun,
>   When first he spreads his orient beams
>   On herb, tree, fruit, and flower,
>   Glist'ning with dew," &c. &c.

You see I am in a perfect rhapsody this morning !— I've begun my song with the birds ; really all nature smiles ; these sons of plunder being driven away, has given life to every thing. O Peace ; smiling Peace ! when will you bless our land with your all-cheering presence ? We want but the assurance of that, to make us a happy people. But, methinks the dear stranger begins

3

to eye us askance ; I hope she will shortly stare us full in the face, and make glad our long-dejected hearts, with all her train of smiling attendants.

*   *   *   *   *   *

But I must continue my narrative, and yet I'm loth to quit so agreeable a subject, to enter on one that was so shocking at the time, and indeed still so,—when I recall it to my "mind's eye." But it is some degree of satisfaction to look back on our sufferings, and congratulate ourselves on their being past, and that they were no *worse* when present. But I will proceed.

As the enemy were moving over to the islands about us, Mr. Smilie quitted Wadmalaw with his family, and removed to a plantation of my Father's, on Stono road ; but he had not been there long before we heard they were encamped at Stono Ferry, not more than seven miles from either of my Father's places. This put us in a deplorable situation again ; I wanted to move more out of the way of them ; but surely, thought I, my Father's venerable aspect and grey hairs will excite compassion at least, and I've no husband to fight against them (though, by the bye, if I had one who refused to enter the field in his country's cause, I believe I should despise him from my soul.) Besides, says I, our weak sex, "*incapable* of wrong, from either side claims privilege of safety." That I quoted from some book or other by way of consolation. Such vain thoughts pacified me for the present, (for *vain* they proved to be.) But after awhile, I could not think of staying at Father's, as he lived on the river, and we very often saw boat-loads of red-coats pass and repass ; so I went and staid with my sister at the plantation. She had another lady with her too ; one Miss Samuells. While we staid there, we used to see parties of our friends—mostly the Willtown hunt-ers, pass the avenue, towards Stono Ferry, where they rode daily in search of adventures, and would frequent-ly call on us. O ! how sweet, how comforting, the pre-sence of a friend in such distressing times ; especially those we look on as the protectors, the prop of their country. And yet, with a tender anxiety for their wel-fare, we beheld them ; the poorest soldier, who would call at any time for a drink of water, I would take a pleasure in giving it to him myself, and many a dirty ragged fellow have I attended, with a bowl of water, or milk and water ; and with the utmost compassion beheld their tattered raiment and miserable situation ; they real-ly merit every thing who will fight from principle alone ; for, from what I could learn, these poor creatures had

nothing to protect, and seldom get their pay ; and yet
with what alacrity will they encounter danger and hardships of every kind !

All this time we had not seen the face of an enemy,
not an open one—for I believe private ones were daily
about. One night, however, upwards of sixty dreaded
red-coats, commanded by Major Graham, passed our gate,
in order to surprise Lieut. Morton Wilkinson at his own
house, where they understood he had a party of men.
A negro wench was their informer, and also their con-
ductor ; but (thank heaven) some how or other they
failed in their attempt, and repassed our avenue early
in the morning, but made a halt at the head of it, and
wanted to come up ; but a negro fellow, whom they had
got at a neighbor's not far from us to go as far as the
Ferry with them, dissuaded them from it, by saying it was not worth while, for it was only a plantation belonging to an old decrepit gentleman, who did
not live there ; so they took his word for it, and proceeded on. You may think how much we were alarmed when we heard this, which we did the next morning;
and how many blessings the negro had from us for
his consideration and pity.

After this, we saw not any of our friends for a great

while ; they had taken a different route to Willtown, Pon Pon, and other places ; where they heard the negroes were very unruly, and doing great mischief ; so they rode about from plantation to plantation, in order to quell them in time. We grew melancholy and unhappy on our friends disappearing, and hourly expected unwelcome visitors ; but seeing nor hearing nothing of them, only that they were erecting forts at the Ferry, I began to be in hopes they would not be so free in obtruding their company on us, as they had done elsewhere ; but at length the time arrived. The 2d of June, two men rode up to the house ; one had a green leaf, the other a red string in his hat ; this made us suspect them as spies (for we heard M'Girth's men wore such things in their hats.) They were very particular in their inquiries " if there were any men in the house ?" (Foolish fellows ! if there were, they would not have had time to have asked us that question.)—" If any had been there ?" " No." " Did any go from here this morning ?" Impertinents, thought I ; do you think that we are bound to answer to all your interrogations ! but I must not say so. " Well," says one, " do you know Col. M'Girth will be along here presently with two hundred men ? You may expect him in an hour or two."

3*

Ah! thought I—I'd far rather (if I must see one) see
old Beelzebub ; but here are some of his imps—the fore-
runners of his approach. " Why," (said my friend, Miss
Samuells,) " if Col. M'Girth should come, I hope he
wont act ungenteelly, as he'll find none but helpless women here, who never injured him !" " O !" says one,
" he'll only take your clothes and negroes from you."
After a little farther chat, they rode off, leaving us in
a most cruel situation, starting at every noise we heard,
and dreading the enemy's approach. In the meanwhile
Father and Mother had two visitors of the same class ;
they persuaded Father to take a protection, but in vain; he
declined it—they then threatened him if he did not, but
withall, assured him, that if he would, such a number of men
should be with him to guard his property. " Then," says
Father, " the Americans will send a greater, and how
then ?" " Why, then you will have such a number," say
they. But Father replied that, whatever number they'd
send, the Americans would still send a greater, and their
guard would be of no service to him. They then asked him
if he'd heard of one M'Girth. " Yes, I've heard of such
a person," says Father. " Did you ever hear any good
of him ?" " Why, no, I can't say I have—people complain very much of him." " Well," say they, " if you

don't take a protection, he'll plunder you of every thing
—he'll be here presently."   " I can't help it," was all the
reply.

Well, now comes the day of terror—the 3d of June.
(I shall never love the anniversary of that day.) In
the morning, fifteen or sixteen horsemen rode up to the
house ; we were greatly terrified, thinking them the enemy, but from their behavior, were agreeably deceived,
and found them friends.   They sat a while on their
horses, talking to us ; and then rode off, except two, who
tarried a minute or two longer, and then followed the
rest, who had nearly reached the gate.   One of the said
two must needs jump a ditch—to show his activity I suppose ; for he might as well, and better, have gone in the
road.   However, he got a sad fall ; we saw him, and
sent a boy to tell him, if he was hurt, to come up to the
house, and we would endeavor to do something for him.
He and his companion accordingly came up ; he look'd
very pale, and bled much ; his gun somehow in the fall,
had given him a bad wound behind the ear, from whence
the blood flowed down his neck and bosom plentifully :
we were greatly alarmed on seeing him in this situation,
and had gathered around him, some with one thing, some
with another, in order to give him assistance.   We were

very busy examining the wound, when a negro girl ran in, exclaiming—"O! the king's people are coming, it must be them, for they are all in red." Upon this cry, the two men that were with us snatched up their guns, mounted their horses, and made off; but had not got many yards from the house, before the enemy discharged a pistol at them. Terrified almost to death as I was, I was still anxious for my friends' safety; I tremblingly flew to the window, to see if the shot had proved fatal: when, seeing them both safe, "Thank heaven," said I, "they've got off without hurt!" I'd hardly utter'd this, when I heard the horses of the inhuman Britons coming in such a furious manner, that they seemed to tear up the earth, and the riders at the same time bellowing out the most horrid curses imaginable; oaths and imprecations, which chilled my whole frame. Surely, thought I, such horrid language denotes nothing less than death; but I'd no time for thought— they were up to the house—entered with drawn swords and pistols in their hands; indeed, they rushed in, in the most furious manner, crying out, "Where're these women rebels?" (pretty language to ladies from the *once famed Britons!*) That was the first salutation! The moment they espied us, off went our caps, (I always heard say

none but women pulled caps !) And for what, think you?
why, only to get a paltry stone and wax pin, which kept
them on our heads ; at the same time uttering the most
abusive language imaginable, and making as if they'd
hew us to pieces with their swords. But it's not in my
power to describe the scene : it was terrible to the last
degree; and, what augmented it, they had several armed
negroes with them, who threatened and abused us greatly. They then began to plunder the house of every
thing they thought valuable or worth taking ; our trunks
were split to pieces, and each mean, pitiful wretch cram-
med his bosom with the contents, which were our apparel, &c. &c. &c.

I ventured to speak to the inhuman monster who had
my clothes. I represented to him the times were such
we could not replace what they'd taken from us, and
begged him to spare me only a suit or two ; but I got
nothing but a hearty curse for my pains ; nay, so far
was his callous heart from relenting, that, casting his
eyes towards my shoes, " I want them buckles," said he,
and immediately knelt at my feet to take them out, which,
while he was busy about, a brother villain, whose enor-
mous mouth extended from ear to ear, bawled out " Shares
there, I say ; shares." So they divided my buckles be-

tween them. The other wretches were employed in the same manner; they took my sister's ear-rings from her ears; hers, and Miss Samuells's buckles; they demanded her ring from her finger; she pleaded for it, told them it was her wedding ring, and begged they'd let her keep it; but they still demanded it, and, presenting a pistol at her, swore if she did not deliver it immediately, they'd fire. She gave it to them, and, after bundling up all their booty, they mounted their horses. But such despicable figures! Each wretch's bosom stuffed so full, they appeared to be all afflicted with some dropsical disorder; had a party of rebels (as they called us) appeared, we should soon have seen their circumference lessen.

They took care to tell us, when they were going away, that they had favored us a great deal—that we might thank our stars it was no worse. But I had forgot to tell you, that, upon their first entering the house, one of them gave my arm such a violent grasp, that he left the print of his thumb and three fingers, in black and blue, which was to be seen, very plainly, for several days after. I showed it to one of our officers, who dined with us, as a specimen of British cruelty. If they call this *favor*, what must their cruelties be? It must want a name. To be brief; after a few words more, they rode

off, and glad was I. " Good riddance of bad rubbish,"
and indeed such rubbish was I never in company with
before. One of them was an officer too ! a sergeant, or
some such, for he had the *badge of honor on his shoulders !*
After they were gone, I began to be sensible of the danger I'd been in, and the thoughts of the vile men seemed
worse (if possible) than their presence ; for they came
so suddenly up to the house, that I'd no time for thought ;
and while they staid, I seemed in amaze ! Quite stupid !
I cannot describe it. But when they were gone, and I
had time to consider, I trembled so with terror, that I
could not support myself. I went into the room, threw
myself on the bed, and gave way to a violent burst of grief,
which seemed to be some relief to my full-swollen heart.

For an hour or two I indulged the most melancholy
reflections. The whole world appeared to me as a thea-
tre, where nothing was acted but cruelty, bloodshed, and
oppression ; where neither age nor sex escaped the hor-
rors of injustice and violence ; where the lives and property of the innocent and inoffensive were in continual
danger, and lawless power ranged at large.

I was interrupted in these thoughts by hearing somebody cry out that there were a number of horsemen coming up the avenue. " Well," said I, " here are more

banditti coming ; but death will I suffer before I'll be
cooped up in this house with them again ;" so out I went,
my sister with me. Miss Samuells, having more resolution, was determined to stay, and see who and what they
were. First came up an old man and two others; she
went to the door. " If," said she, " you are friends, I
beg you'll go away, unless you are able to protect us,
for we have been used very ill to -day by a party who
call themselves British dragoons, (*dragons rather ;*) but
if you are enemies, I can assure you there's nothing
left worth your taking, as the house was plundered this
morning by the party I told you of." The above-mentioned old man dismounted, and said he must see what
was in the house for all that. " Well, go in and see."
She walked out, and burst into tears ; called on my sister and myself to come and endeavor to save what few
things the British savages had left. These were a large
party of M'Girth's men. When I saw they did not behave in that outrageous manner the others had done, I
ventured to approach the house, and went in.

One of the men, seeing Miss Samuells quit the house,
jumped from his horse, and swore we should have nothing
more taken from us. He ran in, and brought the old
man out by the shoulders, who declared vehemently that

he had no intention of taking any thing from us ; and to prove that he would rather give, than take from us, he went to his horse, and loosing a great quantity of yarn, (which I dare say he had plundered,) brought it and gave it to my sister. One of them, who by his appearance seemed superior to the rest, asked if " one Mrs. Wilkinson wa'nt there ?" They told him yes, and looking round to where I sat, he bent himself forward on his horse as if to see me. " Gracious heaven !" said I, " what can the man want by asking for me ?" I was ready to sink on the floor ; however, I put on as resolute an air as I could assume, and stepped forward with " Have you any thing to say to me, Sir ?" The man saw I was frightened ; he smiled. " How far is it, madam, from here to Mr. Morton Wilkinson's ?" " I really can't tell ; it's a great while since I've been there, and I hear he's got a new road to his house." He and another one spoke low. He then said, " But you can guess, Madam, how far it is ?" " Indeed, Sir, I can't." " We've orders," said he, " to burn that house." We all plead for it.

" If you go there," said one of us, " you can't find it in your heart to execute your orders ; there you'll find no less than seven small children ; you could not be so

4

cruel as to turn them out of the house, sure." " Well,"
said he, " we wont go ; women and children can't help
what the men do." " Very true," said I ; " but yet you
see the innocent suffer with those who are termed guil-
ty. Come in the house, and see what destruction they've
made !" They came in—expressed a great concern for
us, and abused the Britons much. "Yes," said they,
" we always bear the blame of these outrages ; but I'll
assure you we take nothing from ladies. Men's apparel,
horses, &c. we do take ; but we wish not to distress women, for they can't help what's done. Those fellows
who robbed you this morning can't have any feeling for
the fair sex, I'm sure." (O rare ! thought I, here's
" high life below stairs" in good earnest.)

There was a man among them who would not come
in, but staid just without the door. They kept their
eyes on him as they spoke, with a smile of contempt.
At last said one of them, "Ladies, do you know that
man's face ?" (pointing towards him.) We looked at
him—he seemed to avoid our eyes ; we soon recollected
the wretch, and cried out, " He was among the dragoons
in the morning." " Very true," said they, " he was so,"
and then shamed him. He was very sullen, and after
that could not give us a good word ; whatever we would

say, he would have some surly answer ready ; the others frowned at him, but that having no effect, they spoke to him, and asked " How could he behave in that manner to us ?" He was silent for some time after.

One of them assured us, if we would let him know what we had lost, he would endeavor to get them for us again ; but as we did not want any more of their company, we declined accepting their offer. He swore that as soon as he returned to camp, he would make a report of the usage we had received, and he was sure the men would suffer for it. (He was as good as his word, for we afterwards heard by some of our men, who were prisoners at the Ferry, that the ill treatment we had met with was talked of throughout the camp there ; and afterwards my sister saw the man who reported it. " Well, Madam," said he, " if it will be of any satisfaction to you, I can assure you I saw one of the men, who used you and the other ladies so ill, receive five hundred lashes for the same." So here was " the devil correcting sin.")

" While the British soldiers were talking to us, some of the silent ones withdrew, and presently laid siege to a bee-hive, which they soon brought to terms ; which the others perceiving, cried out, " Hand the ladies a plate

of honey,"—which was immediately done with officious
haste, no doubt thinking they were very generous in
treating us with our own.   There were a few horses
feeding in the pasture.   They had them driven up.
" Ladies, do either of you own these horses ?"   " No !
they partly belong to Father and Mr. Smilie."   " Well,
Ladies, as they are not *your* property, we'll take them.
It can't be injuring you, you know."   The old man got
on one.   " Why," said Miss Samuels, "that horse can
do you no good, it is very ordinary."   " No matter,
Madam.   I'll take a rebel's horse at any time."   "Why,"
said she, " that poor old creature had better be at home.
He can't be of any service to you."   " I think so too,"
replied he ; " but it is no matter what becomes of him."
" Old man," continued she, " if that was a Tory's horse,
would you take it ?"   "Why, no !"   " Faith, old fellow,"
said one, " I believe you do not mind Whig or Tory, so
you get by it."

" Ah, thought I, I believe you speak the sentiments of
your whole army, from the highest officer to the lowest
soldier."   Nothing but the hope of raising themselves
on the ruin of others, has induced them to engage in
the war against us.   I fear *principle* governs very few,
Interest reigns predominant.

Another poor, meagre looking mortal, with a wound in his shoulder, went into the kitchen, and fell to upon some rice. He told the negroes that he wished he had some meat; and, if he was not afraid of distressing the ladies, he would ask them for some. I mention all these trifling circumstances that you may see with how much more humanity M'Girth's men treated us, to what the Britons did; yet we had a most dreadful account of his gang; that they were worse than savages, and committed every kind of outrage. But let every one have his due, and the merit of a good act.

To tell the truth, they behaved to us more like friends than enemies, when they saw our distress. I do not know whether that moved them to pity, or what. They asked if there were any settlements near us. We told them there were; and begged, if they went to Father's, they would treat him and his family well, and do nothing to distress them: for we heard that the dragoons had plundered his house that morning, and insulted him very much.

"We will not, ladies, we will not; and had you thousands, we would not rob you of a shilling. But what's your Father's name?" "Mr. Yonge." "Yong, Yong," said the before-mentioned busy old wretch; " ah, right,

4*

he is an old Rebel. Why, he is one of the Council."
" You are quite wrong, good man." (I told a fib in the
word *good*.) " My Father, besides his being a man in
years, is very hard of hearing, and consequently un-
fit for that office." " But go," said Miss Samuels,
" if his grey hairs can't excite compassion, I do not
know what will." Away they went to their horses,
when one of them, turning round to me, says, " How
far does — does, (he could not recollect my Father's
name) does Father Grey-beard live from here?" Pray heaven, thought I, neither you, nor any enemies to America,
may live to deserve that appellation. The prayer sa-
vored of cruelty, and was rather unchristian ; especially as we are commanded to pray for our enemies, and
to do good to those who despitefully use us and per-
secute us. It is a hard lesson, and I forgot it at that
instant, when indignation had taken possession of my
heart. But I will here conclude. In my next you
shall have the second part of *British cruelty.* Adieu,
my dear. I am quite tired of this long letter ; but more
of the subject.

ELIZA W.

LETTER IV.

Another body of troops visit Mr. Yonge's plantation. They insult and plunder the old people.

I SEEM to have an inexhaustible fund just now for letter writing; but it will amuse your leisure hours, and that hope encourages me to proceed. Without further preamble, I will present you with another scene, where my Father and Mother were spectators, and also sufferers. It was likewise on the 3d of June that my Father, with an old man who lived a few miles from him, and whose head was silvered o'er with age, (one Mr. Bryant,) was sitting in the Piazza, when they saw a party of men—some in red, others in green, coming up to the house furiously; the moment they arrived, they jumped from their horses, and ran into the house with drawn swords and pistols, and began to curse and abuse Father and the other man very much; indeed, took his buckles from his shoes, searched his pockets, and took

all they found there ; they then went to search Mr.
Bryant's pockets ; he threw his top jacket aside, and
producing his under-one, " Here," said he, " I'm a poor
old man," (he was so, sure enough.) They searched,
but I believe found nothing, for by a lucky thought the
" poor old man" saved several hundred pounds, by carelessly casting aside his top jacket, as if it had no pockets in it.   They then went in the rooms up and down
stairs, demolished two sets of drawers, and took all they
could conveniently carry off.   One came to search Mother's pockets too, (audacious fellow !) but she resolutely
threw his hand aside.   " If you must see what's in my
pocket, I'll show you myself ;" and she took out a thread-
case, which had thread, needles, pins, tape, &c. &c.   The
mean wretch took it from her.   They even took her two
little children's caps, hats, &c. &c. ; and when they took
Mother's thread, &c. she asked them what they did with
such things, which must be useless to them ?   " Why,
Nancy would want them."   They then began to insult
Father again in the most abusive manner.   " Aye," says
one, " I told you yesterday how you'd be used if you did
not take a protection ! But you would not hear me ; you
would not do as I told you, now you see what you have
got by it."   " Why," said Mother, in a jeering way, " is

going about plundering women and children, taking the State?" "I suppose you think you are doing your king a great piece of service by these actions, which are very noble, to be sure; but you are mistaken—'twill only enrage the people; I think you'd much better go and fight the men, than go about the country robbing helpless women and children; that would be doing something." "O! you are all, every one of you, rebels! and, old fellow," (to Father,) "I have a great mind to blow my pistol through your head." Another made a pass at him, (inhuman monsters—I have no patience to relate it,) with his sword, swearing he had "a great mind," too, to run him through the body.

What callous-hearted wretches must these be, thus to treat those who rather demanded their protection and support. Grey hairs have always commanded respect and reverence until now; but these vile creatures choose the aged and helpless for the objects of their insults and barbarity. But what, think you, must have been my Father's feelings at the time! used in such a manner, and not having it in his power to resent it; what a painful conflict must at that instant have filled his breast. He once or twice, (I heard him say afterwards,) was on the verge of attempting to defend himself and property;

his breast was torn with the most violent agitations; but when he considered his helpless situation, and that certain death must ensue, he forbore, and silently submitted to their revilings and insults. It reminds me of poor old Priam, King of Troy, when he says,

> " As for my sons ! I thank ye, Gods—'twas well—
> Well—they have perished, for in fight they fell.
> Who dies in youth and vigor, dies the best,
> Cover'd with wounds, all honest, on the breast,
> But when the Fates, in fury of their rage,
> Spurn the hoar head of *unresisting age,*
> This, this is misery, the last, the worst,
> That man can feel—man fated to be curst."

I think those are the lines ; it is a great while since I read them.

But to proceed. After drinking all the wine, rum, &c. they could find, and inviting the negroes they had with them, who were very insolent, to do the same ; they went to their horses, and would shake hands with Father and Mother before their departure. Did you ever hear the like ? Fine amends, to be sure ! a bitter pill covered with gold, and so a shake of the hand was to make them ample satisfaction for all their sufferings ! But the " iron hand of Justice" will overtake them sooner or later. Though *slow,* it is *sure.*

After they were gone, poor old Bryant began to bless his stars for saving his money, and to applaud himself for his lucky invention ; he was too loud with it ; Father admonished him to speak lower, for, should any of the servants about the house hear him, and another party come, he might stand a chance to lose it after all ; but still the old man kept chatting on, when lo ! another company of horsemen appeared in view : the poor soul was panic-struck, he looked aghast, and became mute : these were M'Girth's men, who had just left *us*. They did not behave quite so civil to Mother as they did to us; for they took sugar, flour, butter, and such things from her ; but not much. These particulars I had from Mother. And now, my dear, I'll conclude here ; I expect company to spend the day, so will defer ending my long story till the next leisure hour, and will then have another epistolary chat with you. Adieu.

ELIZA.

LETTER V.

WHAT a world of vicissitudes is this! The scenes continually changing! It reminds me of a little toy I had once: it was a box with a glass on one side, and by turning a handle, which was fixed in one end, a variety of pictures passed beneath the glass, one continually succeeding another. Some were pleasing, others frightful: one would exhibit a beautiful landscape; directly would follow what was meant ·for an image of Satan, with his infernal crew; another would represent the fine appearance of a " liquid plain," where vessels and pleasure-boats were sailing, and on whose banks the inhabitants of the villas (scattered in view) were walking or fishing; the next would present the sea in a violent storm, and vessels going to wreck by the tempest, with the passengers, mariners, &c. clinging to broken masts, boxes, casks, &c. Don't you think this a picture of the world we live in?

"Alternately transported and alarm'd—
Triumphantly distress'd—what joy! what dread!"

And yet how delighted are we with this same world! We shrink at the very thought of quitting it; we are more taken up with the pleasures it affords, (fleeting as they are,) than disgusted with the dangers and deceits with which it abounds.   But you will conclude I've turn-ed quaker, and the spirit has just moved me to preach you a sermon on the instability of sublunary enjoy-ments.   If I should, my text shall be the fourth chapter of Ecclesiastes, 1st and 2d verses—" So I considered all the oppressions that are done under the sun ; and be-hold, the tears of *such as were* oppressed, and they had no comforter ; and on the side of their oppressors, *there was power*, but they had no comforter, wherefore I prais-ed the dead, which are already dead, more than the liv-ing, which are yet alive."   What say you to my text? Is it not very suitable to the present times?   But I've forgot the narration I was to continue.   Strange I

5

should, when it is the most agreeable part; but it had its sorrows too, as you shall hear.

After having so many unwelcome visitors, we began to wonder what had become of our friends. Here, said I, they have left us to the mercy of those we despise: they have just given us a sight of themselves, and then withdrawn, which makes their absence more painful. We could neither eat, drink, nor sleep in peace; for as we lay in our clothes every night, we could not enjoy the little sleep we got. The least noise alarmed us; up we would jump, expecting every moment to hear them demand admittance. In short, our nights were wearisome and painful; our days spent in anxiety and melancholy.

After a night passed as usual, (in fear and trembling,) we rose; my sister and Miss Samuells left the room before me; and when they went out, six or seven horsemen rode up to the door. They knew them to be a party of our men, as they had been there once before. They told them how we had been used by the enemy; begged them to hurry away, for the enemy were out every day in large parties, and should they come across them, they would be certainly taken. They smilingly answered, " We are enough for them ;" and without saying any thing more, rode off. Being told breakfast was on table, I was coming out of the chamber, with my eyes fixed out of the window, (for I was always on the watch,) when I observed something glitter through a thin part of the wood which bordered on the road. I made a stop, and looked more attentively ; when I soon perceived it to be a large body of men on the march, for their guns kept a continual glitter. They came from the ferry-way, where the enemy were encamped, which made me conclude they were the whole British army coming out against our worthy General; for there seemed such a train, and the glitter of their arms appeared so terrible, I was struck with horror at the sight.— Their number through the woods appeared innumerable. " O !" exclaimed I, in wild affright, " yonder are thousands—tens of thousands of the cruel enemy !" All in the house, both whites and blacks, took the alarm at my outcry. Never was there such a scene of confusion.— Sighs, complaints, wringing of hands—one running here, another there, spreading the dreadful tidings ; and in a little time the Negroes in the field came running up to the house with a hundred stories. Table, tea-cups, all the breakfast apparatus, were immediately huddled together and borne off; and we watched sharply to see which way the enemy (as we supposed them to be) took.

But, O horrible ! in a minute or two we saw our avenue crowded with horsemen in uniform. Said I, "That looks like our uniform, blue and red ;" but I immediately recollected to have heard that the Hessian uniform was much like ours :—so out of the house we went, into an out-house. Upward of forty or fifty horsemen came up. As they were very still and orderly, (which was uncommon in the Britons, at least all who had visited us,) we thought it best to go and see who they really were. Accordingly we went, with fear and trembling.—Great part of them had quitted their horses, and got under the shade of a large tree just before the house door. We went up to them, and began to ask some questions, when an officer came riding up, most of his dress scarlet ; then was I assured it must be an enemy ; but, looking up the avenue, I was half distracted to see it thronged with foot-soldiers. "O !" said I, addressing myself to the officer, out of breath with terror, "who—what are those ?" pointing to the soldiers. "Be not alarmed, Madam, they are our men." Ah, thought I, that is what alarms me ; were they Americans, I should be happy. Just at that juncture, a Negro woman came up, and tapped me gently on the shoulder. "Mistress," whispered she, " I don't like these men ; one of them gave me this piece of silver for some milk ; and I know our people don't have so much silver these times; at least they don't part with it." I thought her remark just, and my suspicions were confirmed.

I then turned around. I looked with horror on the officers and men, as on so many butchers of my country-men and friends. I wrung my hands. I could no long-er contain myself. " O Heavens !" cried I aloud, " I wish I was on some desert island ; but anywhere rather than here." The men started and whispered. I hardly knew what I said. " Why, Madam," said the officer, whose dress was mostly scarlet, " do you distress your-self so ? If you think you can be more secure anywhere else, and choose to go, a party of horse shall conduct you."—And what was my reply, think you, to his kind offer ? Why, quite destitute of all politeness or respect. " I want none of your horse," looking in his face and wringing my hands, and going two or three steps back-wards to get farther from him ; for I was sure of his be-ing a British officer, and conceited he had the most fierce and terrible countenance I ever beheld, (excepting the wretches who robbed me,) and dreaded him more than any of the rest. He kept talking to me, endeavor-ing to pacify me, but all in vain ; he might as well have

5*

bid the ocean be calm in a tempest. The more he spoke, the more I feared him, and the more vehement were my expressions of anxiety. At last he seemed fretted that I would not hear him.—He walked a little way, and returning, whispered to another officer. I was all ear, then, and just heard the last of his speech, which was— " There's several of them out yonder now," making a small motion with his hand towards the place. I immediately concluded that those he spoke of were the before-mentioned small party of our friends, who had not long left us. I then ventured to approach him with, " Tell me, I beg you, tell me what you are going about." He smilingly answered, " Don't be frightened, Madam." But that answer would not do. " I tell you what," said I, " don't fight here : for God's sake, don't fight here ; I can't bear a sight so shocking." " Don't be alarmed, Madam ; don't terrify yourself," was all the reply.

Looking around me, I found we were surrounded by men, and more still coming up the avenue, which increased my concern. Another officer, riding up and seeing our distress, attributed it to the unusual sight of so many men and horses ; for none of them in the least suspected our thoughts. " Take away these horses," said he, " and move ; you create distress." He spoke this

in broken English. Well, thought I, there being enemies is past all doubt ; for that is a Hessian officer to be
sure. The sun being very warm, and I much disordered,
I moved towards the house, which, upon entering, I found
crowded with officers. I made a full stop, and the only
salutation they received was a nod of the head. I am
sure they must have thought me an ill-bred, awkward
creature. I walked to a chair—sat down—got up again
—then resumed my seat. I scarce knew what I did.
Several of the officers strove to pacify me. I gave them
no answer. At length the one I dreaded so much (for
his scarlet and fierce look) entered the house, and began
to comfort me. He took my hand—I withdrew it. My
whole thoughts were with Gen. Lincoln and his army.
Any thing would I have given to have known if they
knew of the Britons (as I thought) coming out against
them.

My sister and Miss Samuells did not suspect them as
much as I did ; that is, they were not so sure, for I had no
opportunity of giving them my reasons, which I thought
very substantial. Miss Samuells chatted to them very
freely, telling how we were robbed, and other things,
which I thought best let alone. They seemed very at-
tentive. Thought I, they are now on the watch for

some unguarded expression that she may let fall, whereby they might gather information of something or other they want to know. I was so vexed with her for holding such an unrestrained conversation with them, that I could have found in my heart to have punished her for it.

One of the officers asked her something, I forget what; but she could not give him a direct answer, so referred him to me. "I know nothing about it," said I; at the same time giving her a most expressive look, with a frown. I was determined they should know nothing from me, let the consequence be what it would; for I did not seem to fear them on my own account: all my concern was that Gen. Lincoln knew nothing of their approach.

Now entered the man whom I supposed to be a Hessian officer; he got pen, ink, and paper, and went into the room, where he scribbled away for some time. The room door was wide open, and he sat right before it; looking up and seeing me, he bowed, and begged I'd step there a little. I had a great mind not to comply—but I will see what he is about with his pen, thought I; so I went to him. "How far, Madam, (in broken English) is it from here to the river?" "Not very far, Sir." "But how many miles?" "I can't rightly guess." "Could

you tell the distance from this place to Stono Ferry?"
"I cannot, indeed." He stopped and mused, putting
down his pen.

Man, thought I, you will not find me so very ready to
answer your round-about questions as you may think for ;
I will sooner bite my tongue off, than designedly or inad-
vertently betray my friends and countrymen; short an-
swers can't lead me astray, and no others shall you get from
me. He took up his pen again.—"But you can tell the
distance from here to Gen. Lincoln's camp?" "I do not
know rightly where his camp is, so can give you no information." Ay, thought I, I now see what all your questions tended to ; you are now come to the point, but you
shall not be the wiser for me, I can tell you that! I turned about to go out of the room, but I found he was not to
be put off so. "If you have a sensible fellow, madam, I'd
be glad if you would send one here." Ah ! said I softly,
now all is over indeed. In the meanwhile somebody, I do
not know who, sent in Father's waiting man, who had just
been sent to us. Ruined and undone ! said I to myself ;
this Negro knows every thing. He then asked him all
the questions he had asked me, but more particular ; and
as he answered, the officer wrote it down. Then was I
more distressed than ever ; a thousand distracting thoughts

came into my head, such as these :—Gen. Lincoln knows nothing of the enemy's approach, nor their real strength; they may be much stronger than he thinks them to be ; and now that he does not expect them, they may be endeavoring to overcome him by surprise and stratagem.

By this man's being so very particular in his inquiries, and writing down all the information he gets, it may be with a design to send large bodies of men to different places. In case our army (being attacked when they do not expect it,) should be obliged to retreat, they may be taken in ambush by some one of their large bodies stationed in different places for that purpose. Then imagination presented our army to view, all carelessly reclined and at their ease, little expecting the enemy would make, or that they were strong enough to make, so daring an attempt; while all of a sudden numbers would pour in upon them from every quarter : then, thought I, will they "die as a fool dieth," not avenging themselves or falling gloriously, but "like sheep for the slaughter." O! how the thought distressed me ! I traversed the room, thinking if I could not by some means prevent this great evil, (don't laugh at me). If I had but a faithful trusty messenger, I would write the General immediately of what is going forward, that he may be prepared to give them a good drubbing.

While I was busy thinking, the Negro, who had given me so much unhappiness by his information, came to me, and told me that some of the officers had asked him if they could not have something for themselves and men to eat, and asked me if he should fetch up two or three beeves. I was quite fretted at the sight of him. " I don't care what you do, nor what becomes of you," said I, (I never was so cross in my life,) several officers in hearing. I then turned to my dismal thoughts again, when Miss Samuells and my sister interrupted me. I told them my fears, and they were very serious about them too. After a little discourse we went into the hall ; just as I entered it, I observed the officer, who had taken so much pains to pacify me, rise from his chair, take his sword in his hand, and look very earnestly up the road ; my eyes followed his, and saw one or two horsemen gal- loping up to the house ; I knew them. Now, thought I, those poor souls mistake these for friends, and are riding up with the greatest confidence that can be ; but surely they would not venture, without being sure who they were ! I then began to be divided in my opinion con- cerning them, and could no longer contain myself; but

running up to the officer, laid hold of his arm. Miss
Samuells got hold of the other, crying, "O tell us, tell us,
whether you are friends, or what ?"

The man gazed upon us with astonishment, (as indeed
all the rest did ; well they might.) "Why, whom do you
call friends ?" said he. "O, Americans ! Americans !" we
replied. "I am, I am an American," (taking us in his
arms.) "We are all friends. Good God ! could I have
thought you suspected us as the enemy all this time,
which distressed you so !" (and he seemed quite affected.)
And now for a metamorphosis, comparable to any of the
famed Ovid's. This man, who but a moment before appeared to me so terrible, all of a sudden was transform-
ed to one of the most agreeable, best-looking men I had
seen a great while :

> "He was, to my conceiving,
> The cheerfullest, best, bravest hero, living."

I then looked round with delight upon my friends and
countrymen ; "my eyes took pleasure to behold them." I
thought it high time to apologize for my rude behavior,
which I accordingly did ; telling them, that as I had not
for a long time seen the face of a friend, I feared they had
all forsaken us, and they, coming up in such a body, and

from the ferry-way too, I concluded they must be the dreaded enemy.

I particularly excused myself to Major Moore, for my rudeness to him in return for the polite attention he paid me. I begged pardon of them all for mistrusting them as I had done, and exclaimed to Maj. Moore, " O Major, that red! that hated scarlet, (pointing to his clothes,) made me suspect you as a British officer, and we have been used so cruelly by *Red Coats*, that I shall never love the color again." " Well," said he, " you shall never more see me in this terrible red. But we have mistaken each other ; you mistook us for Britons, and your distress at sight of us made me conclude we had got in some Tory Family, and that we were very unwelcome visitors. We began to wish ourselves away."—They then laughed heartily at me for my fright, saying, " That they really expected, by the time I had done wringing my hands, I would have no skin left upon them ; but now they knew the reason, they no longer wondered, and were happy to find us at last pacified and easy."

I was quite elated to see such a number of friends all about me ; and you may believe it or not, but every word they said, though ever so trifling, was music in my ear. After the harsh thunder of an enemy's voice, denouncing

6

death and destruction, no wonder that the gentle language of a friend should be harmony. O yes, it was music of the softest and most soothing kind. I felt my bosom glow with gratitude, with affection, for my countrymen. I cannot describe my sensations, but I felt somehow lifted up above myself, if I may so express it.

After a little conversation, I found him whom I had taken for a Hessian officer to be Col. Malmady, a brave Frenchman. The brave and worthy, of what nation soever, claim our esteem and respect. I regard merit wherever I find it, and hope I shall never let passion or prejudice bias me, or make me blind to worth, in whatever breast it may be found; nor would I have you think, that whenever I express a concern or affection for my countrymen, I mean only those who are really so! No. All such as interest themselves in the American cause, and defend their rights and privileges, are my *countrymen*. Do you think I am right? Pray, let me have your opinion.   ELIZA W.

LETTER VI.

Major Moore's thoughts on liberty. Incidents. M'Girth's men
again. Mrs. W. obliged to return to her father's. Incidents on
the way.

AFTER various discourses, the conversation took a turn
on the subject of the present war. I was proud to hear
my friends express themselves in a manner not unworthy
of their country. Maj. Moore made a comparison,
which, as I perfectly remember, I will give you. Your
opinion is also required of the same.

"Suppose," said he, "I had a field of wheat, upon
these conditions, that out of that field I was to give so
much to a certain person yearly ; well, I think nothing
of it, I give it cheerfully, and am very punctual ; it goes
on thus for some years ; at length the person sends me
word I must let him have so much more, for he wants it;
still I comply with cheerfulness. The next year he
requires a still larger supply, and tells me he cannot do
without it. This startles me ! I find him encroaching,

by little and little, on my property. I make some diffi-
culty in complying; however, as he says 'he cannot do
without it,' I let him have it, though I see it hurts me;
but it puts me on my guard. Well, things go on so
for some time; at length he begins again, and at last
seems to have a design of taking my whole field. Then
what am I to do?—Why, if I give it up, I am ruined, I
must lie at his mercy. Is not this slavery? For my
part," continued he, "I would rather explore unknown
regions, blessed with liberty, than remain in my native
country if to be cursed with slavery."

The land of Liberty! how sweet the sound! enough to
inspire cowardice itself with a resolution to confirm the
glorious title, "the land of Liberty." Let me again re-
peat it—how enchanting! It carries every idea of happiness in it, and raises a generous warmth in every
bosom capable of discerning its blessings. O! Americans
—Americans! strive to retain the glorious privilege
which your virtuous ancestors left you; "it is the price
of blood;" and let not the blood of your brave countrymen, who have so lately (in all the States) died to defend
it, be spilt in vain. Pardon this digression, my dear
Mary—my pen is inspired with sympathetic ardor, and
has run away with my thoughts before I was aware. I

do not love to meddle with political matters; the men
say we have no business with them, it is not in our
sphere! and Homer (did you ever read Homer, child?)
gives us two or three broad hints to mind our domestic
concerns, spinning, weaving, &c. and leave affairs of
higher nature to the men; but I must beg his pardon—I
won't have it thought, that because we are the weaker
sex as to *bodily* strength, my dear, we are capable of
nothing more than minding the dairy, visiting the
poultry-house, and all such domestic concerns; our
thoughts can soar aloft, we can form conceptions of
things of higher nature; and have as just a sense of
honor, glory, and great actions, as these "Lords of
the Creation." What contemptible *earth worms* these
authors make us! They won't even allow us the liberty
of thought, and that is all I want. I would not wish
that we should meddle in what is unbecoming female de-
licacy, but surely we may have sense enough to give our
opinions to commend or discommend such actions as
we may approve or disapprove; without being reminded
of our spinning and household affairs as the only matters we are capable of thinking or speaking of with just-
ness or propriety. I won't allow it, positively won't.
Homer has a deal of morality in his works, which is

worthy of imitation; his Odyssey abounds with it. But
I will leave Homer to better judges, and proceed in my
narration.

While the officers were there discoursing, word was
brought that a party of the enemy were at a neighbor-
ing plantation, not above two miles off, carrying provisions away. In an instant the men were under arms,
formed and marched away to the place. We were dread-
fully alarmed at the first information, but, upon seeing
with what eagerness our friends marched off, and what
high spirits they were in, we were more composed, but
again relapsed into our fears when we heard the discharge
of fire-arms; they did not stay out long; but returned
with seven prisoners, four whites and three blacks. When
they came to the door, we looked out, and saw two of
M'Girth's men with them, who had used us so ill; my
heart relented at sight of them, and I could not forbear looking at them with an eye of pity. Ah! thought
I, how fickle is fortune! but two days ago these poor
wretches were riding about as if they had nothing to
fear, and terrifying the weak and helpless by their appearance; now, what a humbled appearance do *they*
make! But, basely as they have acted in taking up arms
against their country, they have still some small sense

left that they were once Americans, but now no longer
so, for all who act as they do, forfeit that name ; and by
adopting the vices of those they join, become one with
them ; but these poor creatures seem to have yet remaining some token of what they once were—else why did
they, last Thursday, behave so much better to us than
the Britons did, when we were equally as much in their
power as we were in the others' ?   I will let them see I
have not forgot it.   I arose, and went out to them.   " I
am sorry, my friends, (I could not help calling them
friends when they were in our power,) to see you in this
situation, you treated us with respect ; and I cannot but
be sorry to see you in distress."   " It is the fortune of
war, Madam, and soldiers must expect it."   " Well, you
need not make yourselves uneasy ; I hope Americans
won't treat their prisoners ill.   Do, my friends, (to the
soldiers) use these men well—they were friendly to us."
" Yes, Madam," said they ; " they shall be used well if it
was only for that."   I asked if they would have any thing
to drink.   Yes, they would be glad of some water.   I
had some got, and as their hands were tied, I held the
glass to their mouths ; they bowed, and were very thank-
ful for it.   I was so busy, I did not observe the officers
in the house ; several of them were at the door and win-

dow, smiling at me, which, when I perceived, I went in
and told them how it was. They promised that the men
should be favored for their behavior to us. " Madam,"
said one, "you would make a bad soldier ; however, if
I was of the other party, and taken prisoner, I should
like to fall into your hands." I smiled a reply, and the
conversation took another turn.

In the meanwhile Miss Samuells was very busy about
a wounded officer who was brought to the house (one
of M'Girth's ;) he had a ball through his arm ; we could
find no rag to dress his wounds, every thing in the house
being thrown into such confusion by the plunderers ; but
(see the native tenderness of an American !) Miss Samuells took from her neck the only remaining handkerchief the Britons had left her, and with it bound up his
arm! Blush, O Britons, and be confounded ! your delight
is cruelty and oppression ; divested of all humanity, you
imitate savages ; neither age nor sex can move compassion ; even the smiling babe suffers by your hands, and
innocently smiles at its oppressor. The Americans are
obliged to commit unavoidable acts of cruelty ; the defence of their country requires it ; you seek their lives
and liberties, and they must either kill or be killed ; yet,

(imitating the all-merciful Creator,) "In the midst of anger, they remember mercy."

> " And will Omnipotence neglect to save
> The suffering virtues of the wise and brave?"

No; I cannot think we shall be overcome while we act with justice and mercy—those are the attributes of heaven. If our cause is just, as it certainly appears to be, we need not doubt success; an Almighty arm has visibly supported us; or a raw, undisciplined people, with so many disadvantages too on their side, could never have withstood, for so long a time, an army which has repeatedly fought and conquered, and who are famed for, or rather *were* famed, for their valor and determined bravery; but now their glory is fallen, and, thank heaven, we are their equals, if not their superiors in the field. I have somewhere read that " vice was the greatest coward in the world, when it knows it will be resolutely opposed;" and what have good men, engaged in a right cause, to fear? When they embarked for America, they were sure of success; for they expected no opposition from a people so little skilled in arms, and who had no experience in the art of war; but to their cost they found, that those who have a true sense of their rights and liberties, will "conquer difficulties by daring to oppose them."

"Heaven's blessings always wait on virtuous deeds,
And though a late—a sure reward succeeds."

Let me read what I have written—my pen is quite unmanageable this morning. I had determined not to make a digression or observation, and before I am aware, it flies from matters of fact or plain narration, and introduces my poor opinion on the stage. What will the men say if they should see this? I am really out of *my sphere* now, and must fly to Homer for direction and instruction on household matters. Begone, pen; I must throw you by until I can keep you in proper order. In good time have I discarded it; for I am this moment called to breakfast. Adieu—another message! Coming —coming.—"Surely, you would not have me break my neck down stairs for a breakfast."

Well, I obeyed the summons to breakfast, worked with my needle, visited; and now again take up my pen; for in the mornings, that is, from sunrise until 8 o'clock, I indulge myself in reading and writing. After that hour I meddle with neither. But let me see! where did I leave off? O! I left at Miss Samuells' parting with her only handkerchief—don't you think her a good girl?

After dinner our friends began to move towards camp ; my brother persuaded us not to stay an hour longer, for the enemy, upon hearing what had been done, might come out, and use us worse than they had done already. Father had the same thoughts, and sent for us ; but having not a horse left, he only sent umbrellas to shelter us from the sun, which was exceedingly warm. My sister packed up a few things, and gave the Negroes to carry, and then we went off. Hard case to us, who had never been used to walking, to walk three long miles in a hot summer's day ; and in such danger too, for as a party of the enemy had just been routed, we did not know but some of them might be lurking about the woods, and the road we were obliged to go was very much frequented by them, so that we walked along with heavy hearts. If we had let the officers know we were going, we should have done very well ; but we had not concluded on it until they were gone. Two of Father's Negro men attended us, armed with great clubs ; one walked on before, the other behind, placing us in the centre.

It was not long before our guard had some use for their clubs ; we were crossing a place they call the Sands, when one of the enemy's Negroes came out of the woods. He passed our advance guard with nothing but the loss of his smart Jocky cap, which was snatched from his head. He turned round, and muttering something, then proceeded on ; when, attempting to pass our rear-guard, he was immediately levelled to the earth ; he arose, and attempted to run off, when he received another blow, which again brought him down. I could not bear the sight of the poor wretch's blood, which washed his face and neck ; it affected me sensibly. " Enough, Joe ! enough," cried I ; " don't use the creature ill, take him at once, I wont have him beaten so." " Let me alone, Mistress, I'll not lay hand on him till I have stunned him ; how do I know but he has a knife, or some such thing under his clothes, and when I go up to him, he may stab me. No, no,—I know Negroes' ways too well." With that he fetched him another blow. I was out of all patience ; I could not help shedding tears. I called out again ; " Inhuman wretch, take the Negro at once, he cannot hurt you now if he would ; you shall not—I declare you shall not beat him so." With that he took him, tied his hands behind him, and gave him to the fellow who went before ; he himself stayed behind with us ; but the poor wretch was sadly frightened. The fellow who had him in custody, walked on very fast, but he kept looking back on us. At last he said to me, " Do, Mistress, let me walk by you." "Don't be afraid," said I, "they shan't hurt you again, I wont let them." But he looked on me so pitifully—his head continually turning round towards me, with such terror in his countenance, that I felt for the poor creature, and, to make him easy, walked, or rather ran, close behind him ; for, to keep up with them I was obliged to go in a half run, the fellow who had hold of him walking at a great rate, for fear of being overtaken by the enemy.

I was ready to faint ; the exercise and extreme heat of the sun overcame me ; but I would not quit the unhappy wretch as he claimed my protection, and my presence seemed some alleviation to his misery ; so on I went, scarce able to support myself. I had got on a great way ahead of my sister and Miss Samuells, when I heard a confused noise, which, echoing in the woods, sounded like lamentations ; my heart was at my mouth. "I'm afraid we are pursued," cried I ; "I think I hear my sister and Miss Samuells crying !" The noise increased ; I made a stop, and was ready to sink to the earth : the Negro, who had the prisoner in custody, heard what I said, and hearing the noise also, took it for granted that we were pursued, quitted his charge, and was making off. I was then some distance behind, for not a

7

step could I take after the stop I made ; when looking, I saw the prisoner standing alone in the path, watching the road very sharply, as if expecting a speedy deliverance. I then found my tongue ; for, thought I, if the enemy should find the Negro in such a bloody condition, they would use us very ill. I called out as loud as I was able to the absconding fellow—" Stop, this moment, and take that Negro ; make all the haste you can with him home, and keep him out of the way ; remember, your life may be concerned in this matter, so take care." The mention of his life was enough ; he grasped the prisoner's arm, and off he ran at such a rate, that they were both out of sight in a minute or two. In the mean time I stood trembling in the road, thinking it useless to attempt getting out of the way, for, so weak was I with the long walk (or rather run), that I could not have gone any distance in the wood if I had ever such an inclination so to do. So, thought I, I may as well die here as anywhere else ; but, upon my sister's coming up to me, I found the noise proceeded from the Negroes with the baggage, who were quarrelling about carrying it.

When they heard, and indeed saw how I was frightened, (for they told me I looked as pale as death,) said Joe, " Do you think if it was so, I'd hab staid behind so

long? Not I! Soon as ever I found how it was, I'd hab
come out before, and that Negro should never hab told
what *hurted* him. I'd have finished him, and got him
out of the way; better for him to die, than all of us die
for him." We pursued our way, and got safe to my Father's, but were greatly indisposed for some days after,
at the end of which we were put in another little flury,
(no end to them, I think,) by three or four horsemen riding
up to the house very fast; but we were relieved from our
fears by hearing one of them call out to us, " Do not be
frightened;" and we found it was Major Moore, with three
of his men. He staid and dined with us, spent a part of
the afternoon, and returned to camp.

He had not been gone long, when a boat-load of *Red
Coats* passed; with them an officer, who stood up all the
way, pointing his hand this way and that, as if asking
whose and whose settlements those were on the river.
In a short time they re-passed, their bayonets fixed, as if
apprehensive of danger. Conscience told them they deserved something for what they had been about; I suppose it was no good.

I see I shall not finish my narrative in this letter; so I
will conclude, and am, as usual, your own

ELIZA.

LETTER VII.

I SHALL give an account of another run we had. Alas!
poor we!—sure never were creatures so bandied about.
One afternoon, my Father, taking a walk in his garden,
observed à boat loaded with men, who, by their appearance, seemed to intend us a visit; he was in great distress at the sight, having been used so ill by them, and
they had sworn they would kill him yet (God knows for
what); he was apprehensive, if they came in a boat, they
would carry him away ; and as he was in a poor state of
health, should they do so, and treat him with fresh insults,
he could not survive it. He came into the house, and shew-
ing us the boat, went down to the landing, and taking
two of his trusty Negro men with him, got into a small
canoe, and rowed up the creek ; the enemy turned up the
creek towards the house. Great was our consternation,

you may believe ; however, we bore it for a while, but could bear it no longer, when we perceived one of them stand up, call to the Negroes who rowed them, to pull hard, and turning from the house, crossed the flats in pursuit of Father ; but he being in a small boat with two excellent oarsmen, they could not overtake him, and getting ashore at a neighbouring plantation, he, with those two faithful slaves, made the best of their way to his planta-tion on Stono road (where Mr. Smilie had stayed) ; he immediately sent off one of them to us, desiring us to quit the island directly, and come where he was.   Indeed, he had no occasion to send, the messenger found us pack-ing up a few things, ready for a march ; but his coming hurried us ; we were soon ready ; a train of Negroes fol-lowing with our baggage, &c. &c.

It was about dusk when we evacuated the Island House, and had three long miles to walk. As I had been obliged to walk it not long before, I seemed a little used to it, and trudged along pretty well; but Mother got quite worst-ed before she was half way, and I believe would have made a night's journey of it if our driver-fellow had not met us with his little nag, and offered it to her. She glad-ly accepted his offer, and, mounting it by his assistance, ambled along *in state ;* while Miss Samuells and I, having

7*

put ourselves in the centre of a crowd of Negroes, who attended us in our flight, footed it away smartly ; but could
not forbear laughing immoderately when we observed to
each other, that if it was daylight, or could we see
plainly, then, what a group of laughable figures would be
exhibited to view. Mother, with her little white palfry,
(it was lame too,) and a gang of Negroes following her,
loaded with one thing or other, excited our mirth. Sometimes we would lose a shoe, which would stick fast under
roots that ran across the path ; at other times we
stumbled over stumps, and ran against each other; for it
was so dark we could not see many yards before us, and
sometimes not at all when we got into a thick part of the
wood. Well, on we stumbled till we came to the Sands ;
the water being still high, it was covered in several
places ; one of the Negro men took hold of my hand to
lead me to those places were the water had gone off. I
suffered him to do so, but finding it very damp, I thought
I might as well go through the water at once, for, said I
" The enemy has caused me two runs already, and I don't
know where I may be obliged to run to before they are ex-
pelled this State, so I may as well begin to inure myself
to hardships at first as at last." No sooner said than done,
through the water went I without a murmur.

It grew late, and the darkness increased ; every thing seemed awful about us, and, what increased the solemnity, the Birds of Minerva kept a continual hooting over our head, which were answered by their neighbors in the surrounding thickets ; and, to complete the scene, the frogs joined their *melody!* and Mother's little girl (whom a servant carried in her arms) would often scream out by wav of *treble,* and I would as often lay hold of its mouth in order to stifle the cry ; and that was instead of the *stops* in music. Here was harmony, my dear ! don't you admire it ? We were serenaded in this *delightful* manner till we got near to the house, and then the dogs welcomed us with a howl. Miss Samuells and myself, with one gang of Negroes, arrived first ; Mother was *jogging* on behind with the other gang. We found Father quite spent with his walk, and much distressed for us, for he knew not but the enemy had been with us. He asked for Mother ; we told him how lucky she was in meeting with a horse, while we were obliged to encounter roots, stumps, and bogs, on foot ; but could not refrain from laughter at the conceit of what a droll figure she must make on her little lame pony. At length she arrived ; we congratulated her on having a horse to ride, but bragged that we had got the start of her though on foot.—" You may laugh (said Mother); but if I had not been so lucky as to have met with the little horse, I should have been foundered, and I don't know but that I am as it is." This set us all a laughing, and sure never were a parcel of runaways in such a merry mood!—And now we could sleep in some security, for we daily saw numbers of our friends, who were continually out, harassing the enemy, and keeping them so penned up at the ferry, that they could not go about committing outrages as they had done; and sometimes in the night parties would ride up, and tell the Negroes to let the ladies know friends had been there, and were constantly riding about the whole night, so they might sleep soundly.

A detachment of two or three hundred men, command-ed by Col. Malmady, were ordered on Father's Island; they had a field-piece with them, and there they staid some time to command the river, which prevented the poor red coats from taking their accustomed airings. When they had been there a day or two, a company of horsemen rode up to the house we were in, and told us the General was coming along, and would be there pre-sently; they had scarcely spoken, when three or four offi-cer appeared in view. They rode up; (Colonel Roberts was with them, he and Father were old acquaintances.) He introduced one of the officers to Father. "General Lincoln, Sir!" Mother was at the door. She turned to us, "O girls, Gen. Lincoln!"—We flew to the door, joy in our countenances! for we had heard such a character of the General, that we wanted to see him much. When he quitted his horse, and I saw him limp along, I can't describe my feelings. The thought that his limping was occasioned by defending his country from the invasion of a cruel and unjust enemy, created in me the utmost veneration and tender concern for him. You never saw Gen. Lincoln, Mary?—I think he has something exceeding grave, and even solemn, in his aspect; not *forbiddingly* so neither, but a something in his countenance that commands respect, and strikes *assurance* dumb. He did not stay above an hour or two with us, and then proceeded on to camp.

That night, two or three hundred men quartered at the plantation we were at. As many of the officers as could, slept in the hall, (the house being very small, and only intended for an overseer's house). We wanted to have beds made for them. No, they would not have them on any account,—" beds were not for soldiers, the floor or the earth served them as well as anywhere else." " And now," said Major Moore, " I'll show you how soon a soldier's bed is made," and, taking his surtout, spread it on the floor—"There," said he, "I assure you I sleep as well on that hard lodging as ever I slept on a feather-bed." —"You may say what you please, Major," (said Miss Samuells,) "but I'm sure a soldier's life is a life of hardships and sorrows." "Indeed, Madam, I think it the best life in the world; it's what I delight in." "I wish all soldiers delighted in it at this juncture," (said I,) "because every thing they hold dear is at stake, and demands their presence and support in the field."

There was one Capt. Goodin or Goodman, (or some such name,) among the officers—I wish I could remember, or rather knew his right name; for he spoke so prettily on the subject, that I've put him down among my list of worthies: I forgot the whole of what he said, but one part I still remember. After speaking of what hardships a soldier necessarily undergoes—"For my part I care not what I undergo," (said he,) "so I could see my country free before I die, and could have this thought to console me in all my sufferings, that I was (in the hand of Providence,) but the smallest instrument in helping to promote my country's welfare; early did I embark in the American cause, and sooner will I die than give it up!" He seemed by his earnestness to speak the very sentiments of his heart.—"May you, and all the friends of

America," (said I,) "soon reap the benefit of your labor; that power which has so long upheld you, I hope will continue to bless and support you, and shortly grant you every happiness you desire." I then recounted to him many of the anxieties and sorrows we had undergone at the time of the enemy's first coming down among us, and how distressed we all were when we could hear nothing of Gen. Lincoln and his army. He seemed quite pleased at the relation. "O, Madam, what men are there that would not undergo any thing when they see and know the ladies are friends to the cause they are engaged in! This prompts us on; we can fight with spirit and confidence, because I'm sure *their* prayers must have some effect; you don't know what concern it has given me when I've found any of the fair sex against our proceedings, but now I care not what I suffer—the thoughts —the *certainty* I may say, that there are some ladies in the world who wish well to an American soldier, will sweeten every hour of sorrow, and arm me with consolation to encounter every danger." Thus far Capt. Goodin—I think that is his name—much more he said which has slipped my memory.—After chatting a while longer we wished them a good night, and retired; and just about day-break they moved to camp.

In the morning a messenger came to Father from the commanding officer at the is'and, advising him to move off his furniture and Negroes, with whatever was on the island that could be moved, as several of the enemy's barges and other boats were coming down the river. Awhile after, we heard our field-pieces begin to roar, and presently an express came along for a reinforcement from Major Pickney, who was a few miles down the Stono road with the first regiment—the reason that a reinforcement was necessary was, that our people were on an island where there was but one passage to go off and on, and that a long causeway; and the enemy might have come through bye-ways from the ferry, and got possession of that pass, which would have proved fatal to our island-ers. A sentry, who was posted somewhere on the main in sight of the river, gave notice that he saw several schooners, which were following the barges; so that it seemed likely the enemy were going to make an at-tempt in force upon them, and they were endeavoring to be prepared for such an attempt. We took one or two boats and a schooner, but no troops from the British came on shore. The next morning Major Wise, and an officer belonging to Col. Horry's horse, breakfasted with us. While we were at breakfast, we heard cannon towards

Stono Ferry roaring in a horrid manner; we immediately quit the table and ran out of doors, to hearken if it was there. We found it was; and for a long time both cannon and small arms kept up a continual awful thunder. With clasped hands I invoked heaven to protect, to shield my friends and countrymen, and was in the greatest anxiety for the event. The two officers who were with us, mounted their horses, and repaired to their posts, and we remained in great distress, our ears still shocked with the solemn sound of what carried death and destruction. We traversed the hall with impatience, yet dreading to hear how it had fared with our army.

At length a soldier entered; rueful was his countenance, (which I believe was natural to him,) and his tattered raiment showed " a variety of wretchedness." He stared me full in the face, giving his head a shake as if it was loaded with what he had to say, and could not get vent enough by speech alone, but required some motion also. This I have since recollected; for at the time I was in such distress I could make no observation. In a hollow voice, he drawled out—" The affair is decided,"—lifting up his hands! By his manner of saying this, I expected no good of our side.

"Explain your meaning," said I; "tell me, how has the battle ended?"

"General Lincoln," (replied he in the same tone,) "and his army are cut to peices!"

This was far worse than I expected; Great God! exclaimed I,—no more could I say, down I sat, overwhelmed with consternation. Imagination soon transported me to the field of battle; there, in heaps, I beheld my slaughtered friends; there did I behold the earth dyed with American blood; there did I also see numbers of wounded, stretched upon their native land in agonizing pain; while the cruel, savage enemy stood insulting over them, and tormenting their already mangled bodies with the bloody bayonet, deaf to all the cries of mercy, and void of every tender feeling of humanity: then would I behold my countrymen expiring in agonies unutterable, while others were dragged away, bound, and treated in the most insulting scoffing manner. And can it be, thought I! is this *really* so?—O day of sorrows! must America indeed fall! after resisting so long too! after so many of her sons have nobly dared to die in her defence, must they die in vain? But I will not trouble you with any more of my thoughts or reflections: indeed, I cannot remember one half of them, they crowded so fast on my mind.

Father and Mother thought it best to get a little more out of the way, so we prepared to do so ; and very opportunely, my brother had come from camp the night before, so Father had his boy's horse put to his chaise, and an acquaintance of ours, to whom I had lent my horse, came with him, and I had him put to my chaise ; and one of Father's horses, which the enemy took from him, preferring the service of a Whig to a Tory, had very faithfully returned home of his own accord ; so we had him for the waiting-man to ride. We were busily preparing for our third run (to Willtown), when two horsemen came riding up the avenue very fast indeed. We called to them, and entreated they would tell us the real truth, though we dreaded to hear the horrid things confirmed. They answered, that they were sent express to the island, and could not stay to tell us ; but the sight of them alone revived my drooping spirits, which were almost exhausted. If our whole army be cut off," said I, "from whence can these expresses be sent ?"

One of them seeing us all at the door, turned his horse and rode up ; the other swiftly pursued his way. No sooner was he near enough, but our mouths were all open to inquire.   " Do, my friend, tell us how the battle has ended ?"   " Why, we have had a smart engagement, and Gen. Lincoln has retreated until he can get a reinforcement from the army."

" Why," said I, " had he not all his men with him in the engagement ?"

" O, no, Madam ; the greater part remains at camp."

One of us expressed our fears that we had a great many killed and wounded, being so exposed to the enemy's shot while they were sheltered by their works.

" I believe," said he, " there are many killed on both sides, for it was a hot engagement ; the shot fell as thick as showers of hail : but I fancy we shall attack them again shortly."

We asked what an express was sent to the island for.

" To order the troops there to retreat to camp immediately, for their number being small, and the situation of the place dangerous, they might be surprised."

This detemined us to hurry off with expedition ; for as General Lincoln had retreated, should the enemy hear that the detachment at the island had done the same, they would fancy they had done some great matter ; and so, flushed with their imaginary success, they would be.

gin to venture out of their lines again to distress the people.

Our horses being ready, away we went, and just got to the road when we saw our little band of Patriots on their march from the island. Several of the officers halted and spoke to us, but did not seem to relish the retreat at all. We rode in company with them a mile or two ; and when we were going to part, an officer in the horse company, observing Father's horse to be none of the best, very politely offered one of his to him, and insisted on his taking it as far as Wiltown. Father thankfully accepted his kind offer ; which was the more kind, we being strangers to him. His servant also attended us, and we soon got to Willtown, where the poor runaways met a kind reception.

And now I think it time to finish this scrawl—I am tired of the pen ; I pray heaven it may never be employed on such a subject again. The country being very dull at present, and most of my friends and acquaintances in town or in distant parts of the country, I had recourse to my pen, and the various scenes of distress I had so lately undergone being uppermost in my mind, I chose that subject to divert my leisure hours, and hope I have

not tired you by the relation ; and now I shall conclude,
ardently wishing, praying, I mean—(Young says,

"Wishing the common hectic of a fool,")

that America, my dear native land, may long, very long,
even to the end of time, be distinguished as the favor-
ite of heaven, and delight of mankind, by a strict adhe-
rence to every Godlike act ; may humanity, piety, and
tender sympathy be the distinguished character of every
son and daughter of America : and may our brethren,
who now sleep in the dust, who expired in defence of their
country, awake at the sound of the last trumpet to everlasting joy and glory; and may we meet them in those
blissful regions of peace and happiness, where no more
oppression can molest and distress us, where the hand of
violence dare not enter, and injustice is not known.

"Hail, sacred Salem, plac'd on high!
    Seat of the mighty King,
What thought can grasp thy boundless bliss?
    What tongue thy glories sing?

Thy crystal towers and palaces,
    Magnificently rise;
And dart their beauteous lustre round
    The empyrean skies.

Bright smiles on every face appear,
    Rapture in every eye ;
From every mouth glad anthems flow,
    And charming harmony.

No scorching heats, no piercing colds,
    The changing seasons bring ;
But o'er the fields, mild breezes there
    Breathe an eternal Spring.

The flowers with lasting beauty shine,
    And deck the smiling ground ;
While flowing streams of pleasure all
    The happy plains surround."

Ah, Mary, who would not wish for a place on those
beautiful shores, especially now that discord has taken
possession of our lower world, and all is dismay and tu-
mult ?   And God knows but in a little time we shall
have a repetition of the same distressing scenes we have
so lately seen acted.   Pray heaven avert it, and restore
peace to this distressed land, and joy to us.

I am, my dear, ever yours.

ELIZA W.

LETTER VIII.

New aggressions of the enemy. Reduction of Charlestown.

SINCE writing the foregoing epistles, we have been humbled to the dust, again plundered, worse than ever plundered! Our very doors and window-shutters were taken from the house, and carried aboard the vessels which lay in the river opposite our habitation ; the sashes beaten out ; furniture demolished ; goods carried off ; beds ripped up ; stock of every kind driven away ; in short, distresses of every nature attended us.

Ah! my foreboding soul! what I feared has indeed taken place. S. Carolina growns under the British yoke ; her sons and daughters are exiled, driven from their native land ; and their pleasant habitations seized by the insulting victors. "Violence and oppression, and *sword law*, spread o'er the plains, and refuge none is found." Those who are suffered to remain, are entirely at their

mercy ; their property is taken and detained from them.
When they complain, they are insulted and laughed at ;
and upon the least suspicion imprisoned, ladies not ex-
cepted, (the Miss Sa——'s, for instance.)   But should I
attempt to enumerate the many base actions which have
attended the reduction of Charlestown—or rather the
capitulation—I should engross too much of my time and
paper ; suffice it to say, that the name of Englishman is a
term of reproach ; they have, by their cruelties and oppressions, cast an odium on their country.   O Britain !
" how art thou fallen !" how are thy virtues, which once
distinguished thee, sunk and swallowed in vice !   Though
I have been a sufferer and sharer in the general calamity thou hast brought on our land, I still lament thee !   O
Britain, I still pity thy disgrace.   A brave and generous
people can never be overcome but by acts of generosity.
Had you endeavored to conquer in that way, we should
ere this have been united in bonds of friendship and happiness ; but, by repeated and manifold injuries, the spirit
of resentment and opposition will subsist.

LETTER IX.

Complaints respecting the parole.

I HAVE this moment received and perused your epistle, and am glad to find your spirits still so good amidst all this trouble and consternation. I saw my brother on Thursday last; I think he seemed more thoughtful than usual. I cannot say I like your paroles at all, for I find by my brother's, that neither your *person* nor *property* is secure,—the one from insult, the other from the hand of injustice. Besides, you have just given yourselves up prisoners at discretion, without the least condition ; surely you could not have considered this matter as seriously as the case required ; if you will reflect, you will find more evil in it than you are aware of. However, I hope the all-wise Disposer and Director of events will turn it to your advantage. In my humble opinion, all such as were of your way of thinking should have kept out of the way, or never put their hands to sign their own dooms. Indeed, you should have parlied, as that parole was in no way satisfactory.

I am now at my brother Frank's, where I spend this day, it being the anniversary of his son's birth. Alas! poor infant, it may be better you had never seen the light; for in such perilous times who knows what your sufferings may be! Do you think I did not shed tears when I was invited here this morning on the occasion? It brought a train of melancholy ideas to view, and sorrowful suppositions; but no more of this, I must end. Company here, and no place I can retire to. Adieu, Adieu! says your Cousin.

Eliza

LETTER X.

Lament over British successes.   Small-pox.

Mount Royal, May 19, 1781.

"Hang dull life , 'tis all a folly,
Why should we be melancholy ?"

Aye, why should we ?   Does it answer one good purpose ? or will it be any alleviation to our present misfortunes ? No.   Very well, then, I will e'en banish it,
and make the best of what I cannot prevent.   To indulge
melancholy, is to afflict ourselves, and make the edge of
calamity more keen and cutting; so I will endeavor to
maintain a calm, let what will happen.   I will summon
philosophy, fortitude, patience, and resignation to my
aid ; and sweet hope, which never forsakes us, will be
one chief support.   Let us, by anticipation, be happy ;
and though we may have cause to mourn, let it not be
with despair.

I have just got the better of the small-pox, thanks be to God for the same. My face is finely ornamented, and my nose *honored with thirteen spots.* I must add, that I am pleased they will not pit, for as much as I revere the number, I would not choose to have so conspicuous a mark. I intend, in a few days, to introduce my spotted face in Charlestown. I hear there are a number of my friends and acquaintances to be exiled, and I must see them before they are. Oh! Mary, who can forbear to execrate these barbarous, insulting *red-coats?* I despise them most cordially, and hope *their* day of suffering is not far off. I have received a long epistle from on board the prison ship; it is dated from the "Pack Horse, or Wilful Murder," and signed by two of its inhabitants. They first congratulate me on my recovery from the small-pox, and then proceed to a detail of their sufferings, and a description of their present habitation. But I am very much pleased to see by their style, that they bear all with fortitude, and are still in high spirits. I have also had a letter from Capt. ****; he advises me to take care whom I speak to, and not to be very saucy; for the two Miss Sarazens were put in Provost, and very much insulted for some trifle or other. Did you ever hear the like! Do the Britons imagine that they will conquer

America by such actions ? If they do, they will find themselves much mistaken. I will answer for that. We may
be *led*, but we never will be *driven !* He also writes me,
that the Britons were making great preparations to cele-
brate the anniversary of the day that Charlestown ca-
pitulated, and that, what with the *grand parade*, and one
thing or other, a poor rebel had not the least chance to
walk the streets without being insulted ; but, in opposition to all that, he had hoisted a very large *union* in his
hat, and would brave it out ; that the rebel ladies were
obliged to compose their phizzes before they dared to
venture in the streets ; and concludes in as high spirits
as he began. How it pleases me to see our prisoners
bear it as they do. They live in the greatest harmony
together, and are in high favor with the ladies ; which, I
dare say, gives the proud conquerors the heart-burn.
Bless me ! here is a whole troop of British horse coming
up to the house ; get into my bosom, letter ;—how I trem-
ble ! I won't finish it until I return from Charlestown.
Adieu, till then.

LETTER XI.

Mrs. Wilkinson visits Charlestown. Goes on board the prison-ship. Conversation with British Officers. Walk on the Bay. Shopping in Broad Street.

YONGE'S ISLAND, July 14th.

WELL, I have been to town, and seen all my friends and quarrelled with my enemies. I went on board the prison ship, too, and drank coffee with the prisoners; the dear fellows were in high spirits, and expecting to be speedily exchanged; indeed, they were so before I left town. I saw the last vessel sail, and a number of ladies with them of our acquaintance, who have sailed from their native land. The day that the last vessel sailed, some British officers came to the house where I staid. I was sitting very melancholy, and did not alter my position on their entrance. They sat for some time; at length they broke silence with—"You seem melancholy, Madam!" "I am so, Sir; I am thinking how suddenly I am deprived of my friends, and left almost alone in the midst of "——

"Do not say enemies, Madam," (interrupting me,)—
"there is not one in this garrison but would protect and
serve you to the utmost of his power, as well as those
whose absence you lament."

"I have no further business in this garrison, Sir; those
on whose account I came down are now gone, and I shall
very shortly return to the country; or you may send me
off, too—will you?"

"No, no, Madam; I will enter a *caveat* against that—I
am determined to convert you."

"That you never shall, for I am determined not to be
converted by you."

"Why, then, you shall convert me."

"I shall not attempt it, Sir"—and I turned about, and
spoke to a lady by me. Some time after I was asked to
play the guitar,—"I cannot play, I am very dull."

"How long do you intend to continue so, Mrs. Wilkinson?"

"Until my countrymen return, Sir!"

"Return as what, Madam?—*prisoners* or *subjects?*"

"As *conquerors!* Sir."

He affected a laugh. "You will never see that,
Madam."

"I live in hopes, Sir, of seeing the thirteen stripes

hoisted, once more hoisted, on the bastions of this garrison."

"Do not hope so; but come, give us a tune on the guitar."

"I can play nothing but rebel songs."

"Well, let us have one of them."

"Not to-day—I cannot play—I will not play; besides, I suppose I should be put into the *Provost* for such a *heinous crime.*"

"Not for the world, Madam; you never should be put there."

"Aye, aye, so you say; but I see no respect shown;" and, saying this, I went into the chamber, and he down stairs.

I have often wondered, since, I was not packed off too, for I was very saucy, and never disguised my sentiments.

"One day Kitty and I were going to take a walk on the Bay to get something we wanted. Just as we had got our hats on, up ran one of the Billets into the dining-room, where we were,—

"Your servant, ladies,"—

"Your servant, Sir."

"Going out, ladies?"

" Only to take a little walk."

He immediately turned about, and ran down stairs, I guessed for what.

Kitty, Kitty, let us hurry off, child ; he is gone for his hat and sword as sure as you are alive, and means to accompany us." We immediately caught up our silk gowns to keep them from rustling, and flew down stairs as light as we could, to avoid being heard. Out of the street door we went, and I believe ran near two hundred yards, and then walked very fast. Looking behind, we saw him at some distance, walking at a great rate. We hurried down another street, and went in a half-run until we came to Bedon's Alley, and, turning that, we walked on leisurely to rest ourselves. It was near an hour after, being in a store in Broad-Street, that we saw him pass, in company with five or six other officers, with one of whom he was hooking-arms.—Kitty spied him out, and, pointing to him and, looking at me, we ran behind the door to hide ourselves ; but he got a glimpse of us before we could do so, and quitting his companions, came immediately into the store, and seemed quite transported to find us. Foolish fellow ! I could not help pitying him for his good-nature, and behaving *mighty civil* to him. Had he been one of your impudent, blustering red-coats, who think nothing bad enough they can say of the *rebels*, I should have discarded him that mo- ment, and driven him from my presence; but he ac- costed us so smilingly, and with such an air of diffience a that I could not find in my heart one spark of ill-nature towards him; so I smiled too, and away we walked. He offered me his hand, or arm rather, to lean on.

"Excuse me, Sir," said I; "I will support myself, if you please."

"No, Madam, the pavements are very uneven—you may get a fall; do accept my arm."

"Pardon me. I cannot."

"Come, you do not know what your condescension may do—I will turn rebel!"

"Will you? said I, laughing—"turn rebel first, and then offer your arm."

We stopped in another store, where were several Bri- tish officers; after asking for articles which I wanted, I saw a broad roll of ribbon, which appeared to be of black and white stripes.

"Go," said I to the officer that was with us, "and reckon the stripes of that ribbon; see if they are *thirteen!*" (with an emphasis I spoke the word—and he went too!)

"Yes, they are thirteen, upon my word, Madam."

" Do hand it me." He did so ; I took it, and found that it was narrow black ribbon, carefully wound round a broad white. I returned it to its place on the shelf.

" Madam," said the merchant, " you can buy the black and white, too, and tack them in stripes."

" By no means, Sir ; I would not have them *slightly tacked*, but *firmly united*." The above-mentioned officers sat on the counter kicking their heels ;—how they gaped at me when I said this ! but the merchant laughed heartily.

Well, I have composed a long letter out of nothing ; pardon the subject. I am on this lonely island, and have nothing to inspire my pen. Let me hear from you, but I would rather see you, if you would think it worth while to favor me with a visit. Come, my dear, I have a thousand little things to whisper in your ear, of *who*, and *what*, and *how*. If you have but the tenth part of that curiosity ascribed to your sex, you will fly to Yonge's Island, to *enjoy* these promised tete-à-tetes.—Not one word more.

Eliza W.

LETTER XII.

" Hark!—the joyful news has come!"

YES, joyful indeed! Cornwallis—the mighty British hero—the man of might and his boasted army, are conquered, subdued, by the glorious Washington! Ten thousand blessings on the name,—May heaven always crown his endeavors with the like success :—but that is not all the "joyful news!" my dear; General Greene with his army are crossing Santee River, and we shall shortly have him here among us : and then how happy we shall be, surrounded by friends, and saying and doing what we please without fear of punishment. Our *red* and *green birds,* who have been, for some time past, flying about the country, and insolently perching themselves upon our houses, will be all caged up in Charlestown :—that is the beauty of it !—Oh, how they will flutter about, and beat their plumes in mere fright !—Do

you not think it a little spiteful to laugh at them? I
cannot help it ;—I must, I will ; and I have even ventured to laugh at some to their faces, out of a little
sweet revenge—I will tell you all how it was. Mrs.
Fabian has been staying with us for some time. Having been from home longer than she expected, she pro-
posed taking a ride to see how matters had gone on in
her absence, and I offered my attendance ; so the next
morning we attempted to go. We had gone a little
beyond my brother Frank's, merrily talking and laughing, and lo! to our great consternation, we beheld six
dragoons galloping towards us. They commanded us to
" halt," but Mrs. F. n ,t knowing what she said, commanded the servant to " drive on."—He was preparing to
obey her, giving the horse a lash, when the cry of " halt"
was repeated ; and immediately we saw what almost deprived us of sense, motion, nay, life itself,—an army of
red and green coats, both horse and foot ! " Lord help
us, Mrs. Fabian." " What shall we do, Mrs. Wilkinson?"
—we both cried at once, grasping each other's hand,
and never were poor creatures in a more mortal fright.
They came up ; the officers politely bowed, and asked us
where we were going, from whence we came ?—and we
had the same questions to answer to each commanding

officer of the different companies as they passed us :
which, before we had half done, I recovered my reason
and sauciness at once, and gave them a look which said,
"You are impertinently curious ; what is it to you from
whence we came or whither we go." The last company
turned us back. Col. Allen, who commanded the whole,
was with them ; he himself took our reins, and turned the
chaise, politely asking our leave, and telling us we had
best be at home at such a time. " Sir, you will not have
our horses taken from us ?"

" By no means, Madam."

And we did so " sir" and "madam" each other. We
rode along in state,—a grand escort !—till we came in
sight of the house ; when Col. Allen, a considerate, cle-
ver fellow, though among the red-coats, ordered the men
to halt, and would not let one of them approach the house
till he rode up, helped us out of the chaise, and begged
Mother to have her poultry, and whatever else she valued,
locked up, that they might be secured from the soldiery,
and put a sentry over the kitchen, &c. &c. He then
went over to my brother's, where he, and the greater part
of his men, quartered, about a mile from Mother's ; but
before he went, he called a Capt. Sanford, and commend-
ed us and ours to his care and protection ; at the same

time saying to us, " Ladies, do not be under any apprehen-
sion ; I leave you to the care of Capt. Sanford, one of
the *best-bred men in Europe*."

Sanford seemed inclined to worship him for the com-
pliment ; he made a very profound congee, and then entered the house to take charge of us ; but first went and
smarted himself up so fine and so trim ;—his head
combed and powdered with elegance : he came strutting
in, and took a seat by me, and seemed desirous of begin-
ing a conversation, but at a loss for a subject.   At last,
after stroking down his ruffles and fingering his cravat
or stock, he began :   " This is a very pleasant situation,
Miss," I was nothing but Miss for some time.   " Yes, Sir,"
the prospect is agreeable, but the situation I think soli-
tary."   " I do not know, I admire it much, though it seems
rather sequestered.   Do you spend all the year here, or
some part of it in Charlestown ?"

" I used to spend the sickly months, which are our
autumns, in Charlestown, but this year I have resided
wholly in the country.

" But why so, Miss ; you ought to be down now, there
is nothing going forward but concerts assemblies, and
other polite amusements, which ladies generally admire."

I have had invitations to share in them, but have de-

clined, as I would rather be where I am, than in Charlestown just now." We had a great deal of chit chat, but
were interrupted by a little girl of mine, who came to
tell me that the soldiers had cut my homespun out of
the loom, and were bundling it up. " Why, Capt. Sanford," said I, " you command a gang of them. Pray make
them deliver the cloth. Your countrymen will not let
us have Negro cloth from town, for fear the *rebels* should
be supplied ; so we are obliged to weave." He and another officer ran out. I went to the piazza, and ordered
one of the servants to go immediately and bring the
cloth in the house, and have it locked up. She did so,
and the officers who went in quest of it, followed. At
the same time a hog came running across the yard on
three legs ; some of the soldiers were in pursuit of him;
they had cut off the other leg. " Capt. Sanford," said I,
" every thing here was left in your protection." Then
putting on a very grave look, I called to my boy, and
ordered him to drive up the hogs, and carry them up
stairs into my chamber, pigs and all ; saying I would
protect them myself. The sentry, who was at the house
door, laughed ; Capt. Sanford smiled, yet affected to be
in a passion, and, drawing his sword, ran out after the
soldiers. They had killed two or three of the hogs, but

10

he threatened them if they killed another ; so they became
more orderly; then leaving him, I went into the chamber
where Mrs. Fabian and her daughter were, and there I
staid for some time. He walked about the hall, and
seemed very restless ; and Mother going out, he inquired
who I was, and seemed very much taken with me, and
had the assurance to beg Mother's interest in his favor.
At last he begged I would come out, and oblige them
with my company ; I sent him word I was otherwise
engaged, and could not come.

At supper, when saying how long they had been about
our neighborhood, some of the officers expressed their
surprise that they had not been attacked by the
rebels. " Aye," said Sanford, " I wonder at it. We have
been at Willtown, Pon Pon, &c. &c. driving off cattle
and provisions, and they cannot afford to prevent our
doing so. Pray, Madam," to me, " can you tell me what
it is owing to ? Whether from the want of courage or
conduct ?"

" From neither," Sir ; " but as they can take *whole ar-
mies*, they don't think it worth their while to attack a
detachment."

" May be," says one, whose name was Rollinson, "they
have sent an express to Congress to know whether they

must fight us, and are waiting for his return before they do so.''

" Very likely" and " may be so" was re-echoed, and then a hearty laugh crowned the witty speech ; Rollinson laughing louder than the rest at his own sagacity. A deal of *small chat* ensued, some highly ridiculous; but I have recited enough, and shall only tell you, that after we were tired out with the several topics of conversation, they introduced that of the king, queen, and royal family. How the king bowed to one of them, the queen smiled at them while they were on guard somewhere near the royal palace ; and that the royal family were, most of them, near-sighted, as the king himself was. I have repented that I did not say he must have been *very* near-sighted, or he could not have begun this war : for any one who could see at a distance, must have seen the evils which have ensued. We retired to our chambers, and they shall have the credit they deserved for behaving exceedingly well the whole night. We heard not the least noise or riot after we left them, though they had a cask of rum, which they had brought with them. In the hall they kept a profound silence ; and we enjoyed undisturbed repose. They moved early in the morning. Sanford opened the staircase door, and called to me, "God bless you, Mrs. Wilkinson, I wish you every happiness; but do not think you shall stay on this island long. I intend to get an order, and will come and carry you off." After blessing me again, away he went. Wishing you the blessing he wished me, I bid you farewell. And so I conclude.

ELIZA W.

THE END.